BILLIE EILISH

FOR BEGINNING PIANO SOLO

Cover photo © ZUMA Press, Inc. / Alamy Stock Photo

ISBN 978-1-70513-107-7

Visit Hal Leonard Online at
www.halleonard.com

Contact us:
Hal Leonard
7777 West Bluemound Road
Milwaukee, WI 53213
Email: info@halleonard.com

In Europe, contact:
Hal Leonard Europe Limited
42 Wigmore Street
Marylebone, London, W1U 2RN
Email: info@halleonardeurope.com

In Australia, contact:
Hal Leonard Australia Pty. Ltd.
4 Lentara Court
Cheltenham, Victoria, 3192 Australia
Email: info@halleonard.com.au

BAD GUY

Words and Music by BILLIE EILISH O'CONNELL
and FINNEAS O'CONNELL

Moderately fast

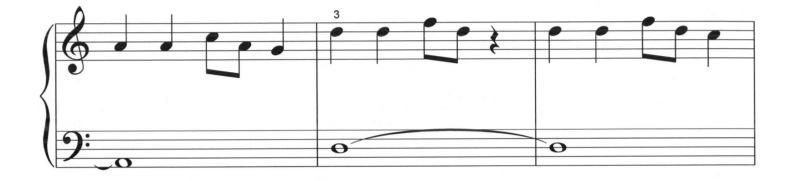

White shirt now
I shirt like

red: my blood-y nose.
when you take con-trol.

Sleep-ing, you're
E - ven if

on your tip-py toes,
you know that you don't

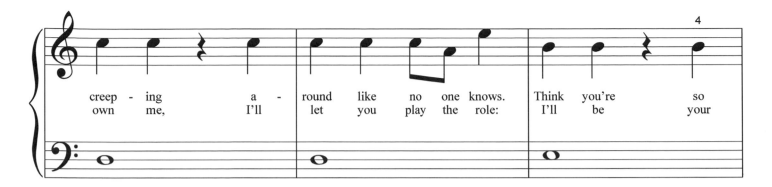

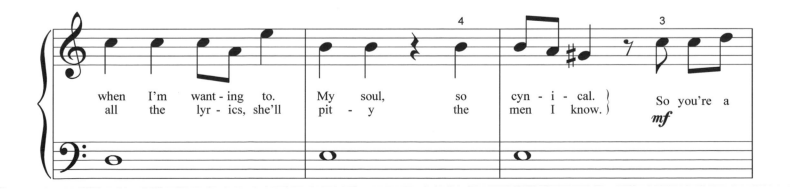

tough guy, "I like it real-ly rough" guy, "I just can't get e-

nough" guy, "chest al-ways so puffed" guy. I'm that bad type, "make your ma-ma

sad" type, "make your girl-friend mad" type, "might se-duce your

dad" type. I'm the bad guy. _____ Duh.

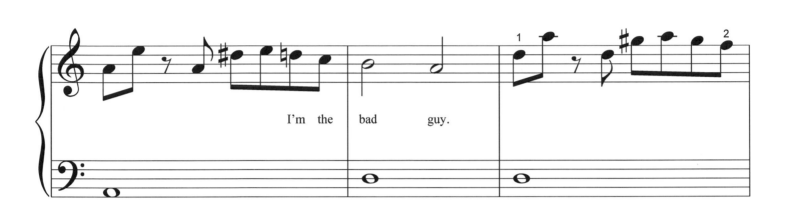

I'm the bad guy.

OCEAN EYES

Words and Music by
FINNEAS O'CONNELL

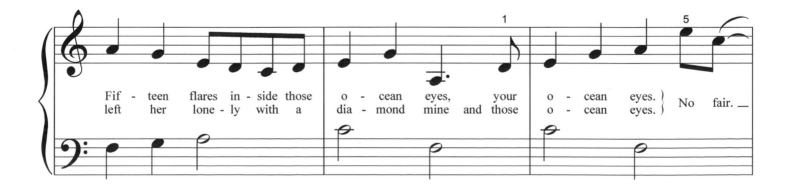

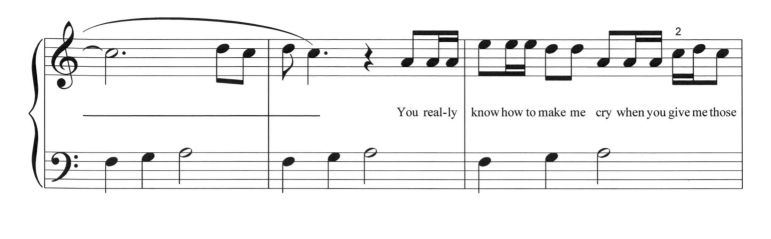

You real-ly know how to make me cry when you give me those

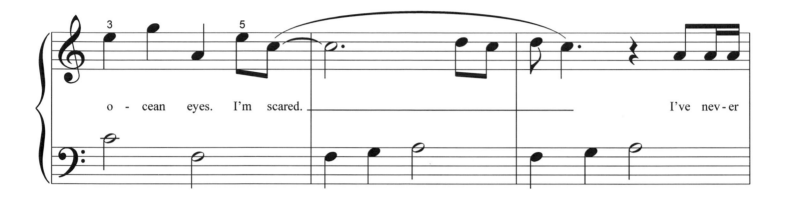

o - cean eyes. I'm scared. I've nev - er

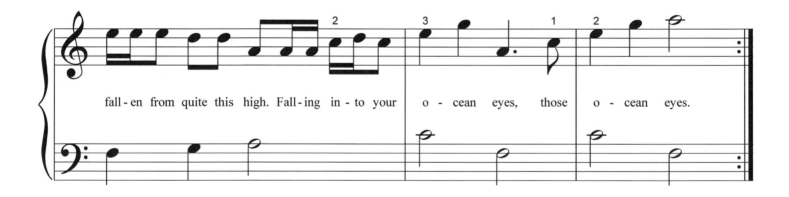

fall - en from quite this high. Fall-ing in - to your o - cean eyes, those o - cean eyes.

(Vocal ad lib.)

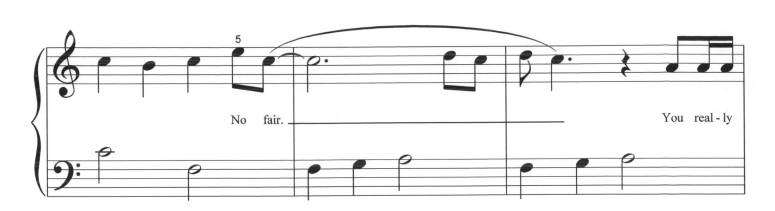

No fair. _____ You real-ly

know how to make me cry when you give me those o - cean eyes. I'm scared. _

_____ I've nev - er

fall - en from quite this high. Fall-ing in - to your o - cean eyes, those o - cean eyes.

COME OUT AND PLAY

Words and Music by BILLIE EILISH O'CONNELL
and FINNEAS O'CONNELL

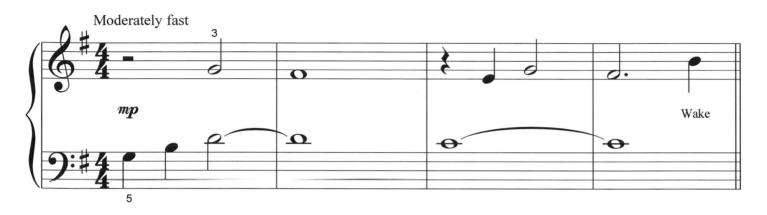

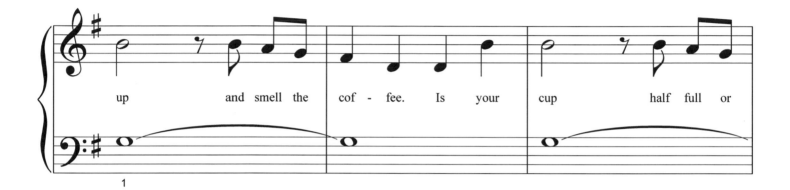

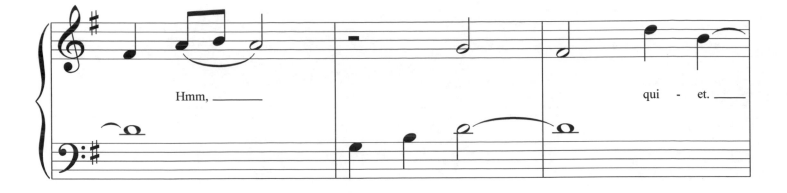

Hmm, _____ qui - et. _____

_____ Hmm, _____ You

see a piece of pa - per; could be a lit - tle
up, out of your win - dow. See snow; won't let it

1

great - er. Show me what you could make her. You'll
in, though. Leave home and feel the wind blow, it's

nev - - er know un - til you try it. ____
cold - - er here in - side in si - lence. ____

Hmm, ____

and you don't have to keep it qui - et. ____
And you don't have to keep it qui - et. ____

And I
Yeah, I

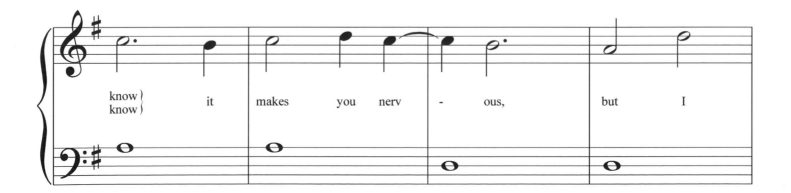

know }
know } it makes you nerv - ous,   but I

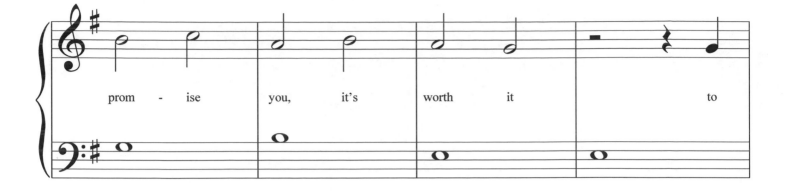

prom - ise   you,   it's   worth   it   to

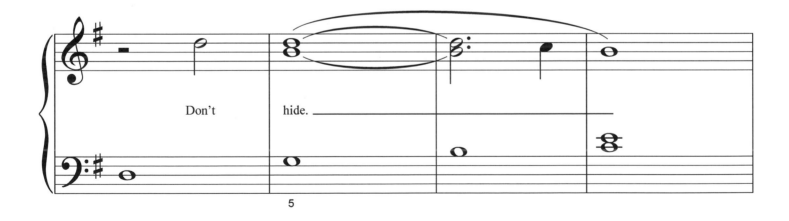

show 'em ev - 'ry - thing   you   kept ___   in - side.

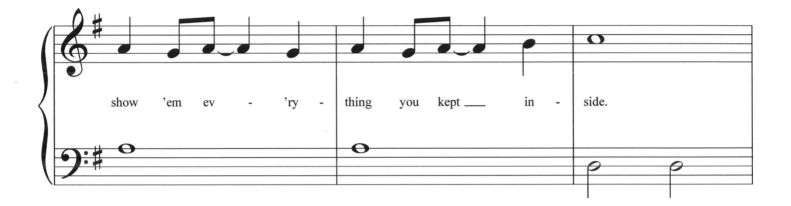

Don't   hide. _____

5

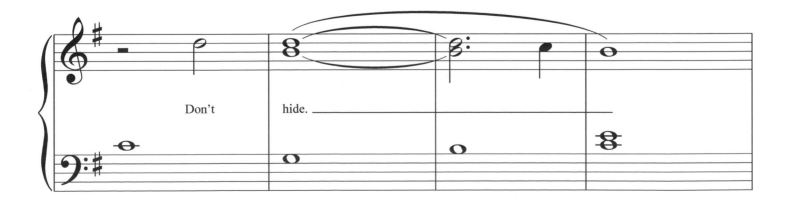

Don't   hide. _____

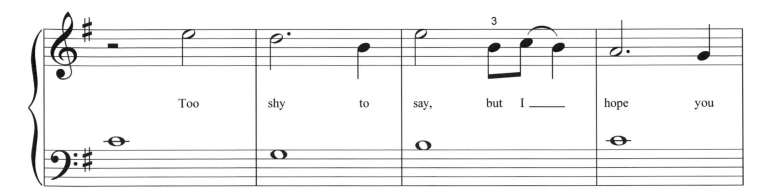

Too shy to say, but I _____ hope you

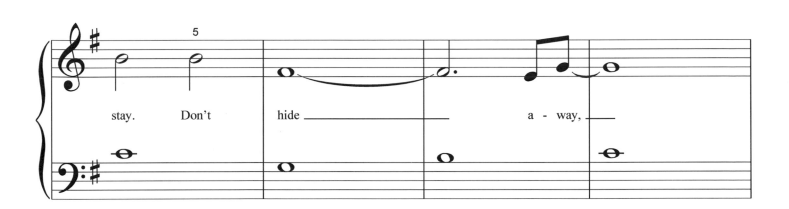

stay. Don't hide _____ a - way, _____

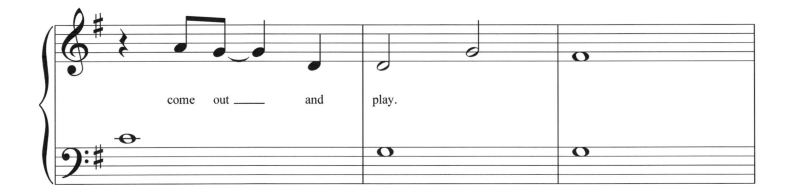

come out _____ and play.

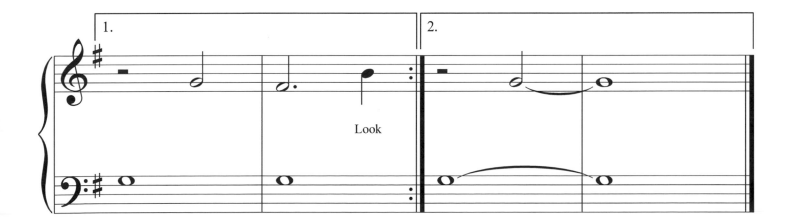

Look

EVERYTHING I WANTED

Words and Music by BILLIE EILISH O'CONNELL
and FINNEAS O'CONNELL

Moderately fast

I had a dream
Thought I could fly,

I got ev - 'ry - thing I
so I stepped off the

want - ed.
Gold - en.

Not what you'd
No - bod - y

think,
cried,

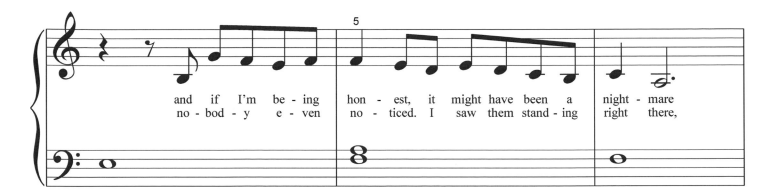

and if I'm be - ing honest, it might have been a night - mare
no - bod - y e - ven no - ticed. I saw them stand - ing right there,

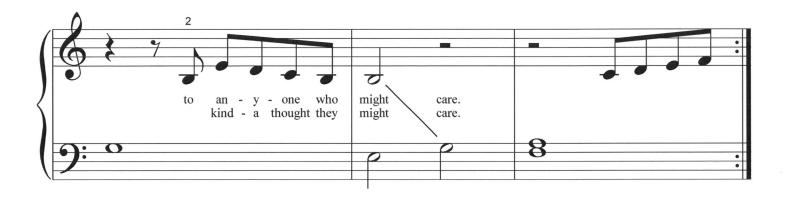

to an - y - one who might care.
kind - a thought they might care.

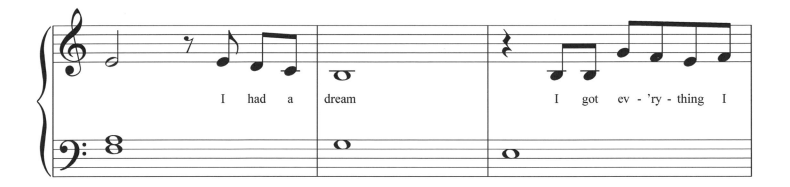

I had a dream I got ev - 'ry - thing I

want - ed. But when I wake up, I see you with

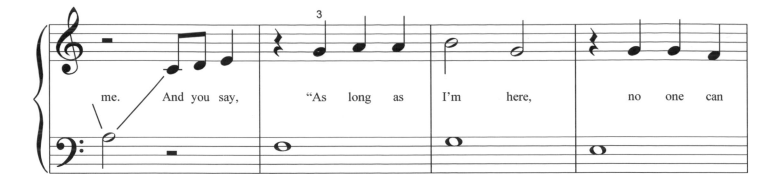

me. And you say, "As long as I'm here, no one can

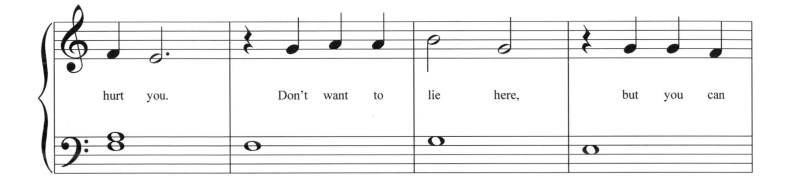

hurt you. Don't want to lie here, but you can

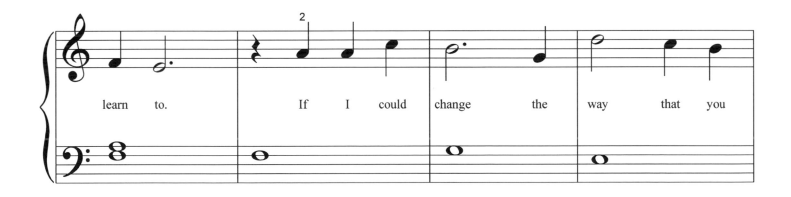

learn to. If I could change the way that you

see your - self, you would-n't won - der why you're here. They don't de -

serve you."   If I knew it all   then, would I   do it a -

gain, would I   do it a - gain?   If they knew what they

said would go straight to my   head, what would they say in - stead?

LOVELY

Words and Music by BILLIE EILISH O'CONNELL,
FINNEAS O'CONNELL and KHALID ROBINSON

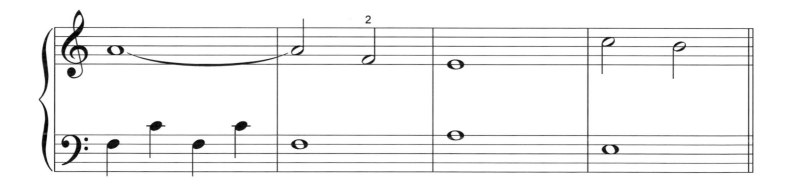

Thought I found a way,
Walk-ing out of time,

thought I found a way out.
look-ing for a better place.

But you nev - er go a - way, so I
Some-thing's on my mind,

guess I got - ta stay now. Oh, I hope ___ some - day I'll
al - ways in my head space. But I know ___ some - day

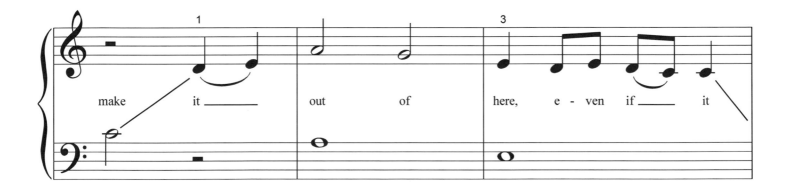

make it ___ out of here, e - ven if ___ it

takes all night or a hun - dred

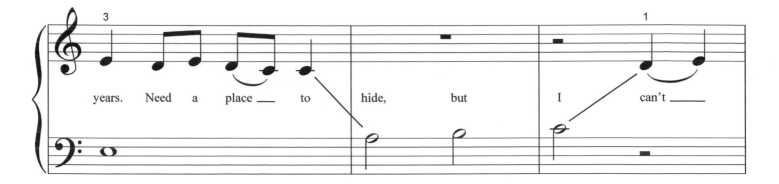

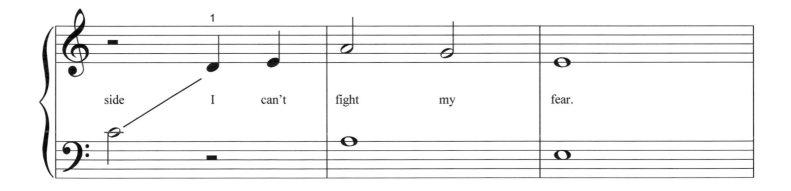

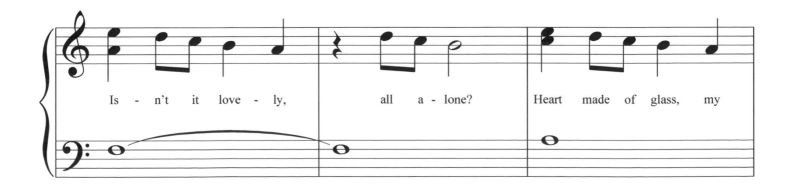

mind of stone. Tear me to piec - es, skin to bone.

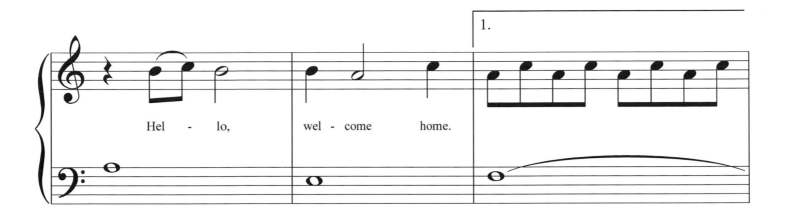

Hel - lo, wel - come home.

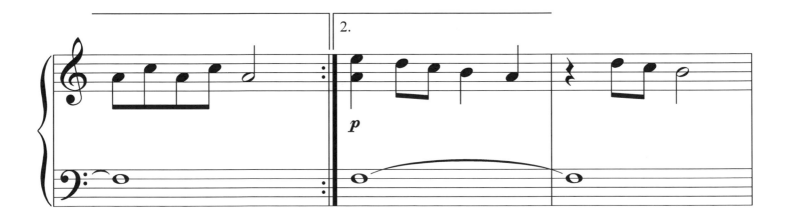

Hel - lo, wel - come home.

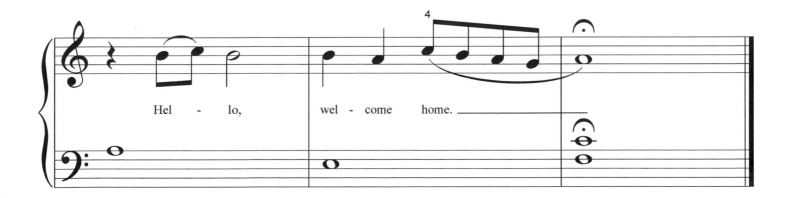

Hel - lo, wel - come home.

MY FUTURE

Words and Music by BILLIE EILISH O'CONNELL
and FINNEAS O'CONNELL

Slowly, in 2

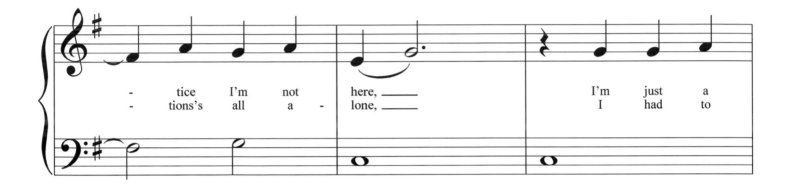

Do you un - der - stand? _____ I've

changed my plans. 'Cause I, _____

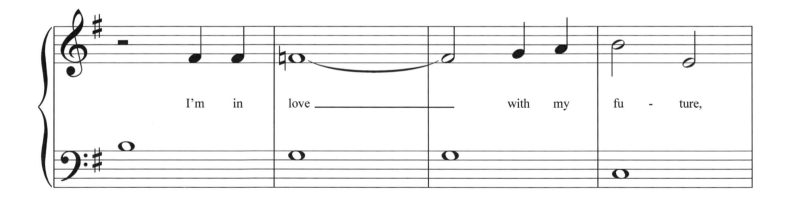

I'm in love _____ with my fu - ture,

can't wait to meet her. _____ And

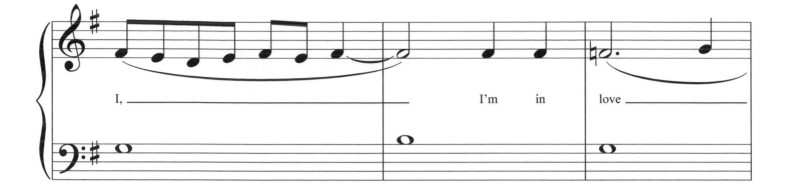

I, _____ I'm in love _____

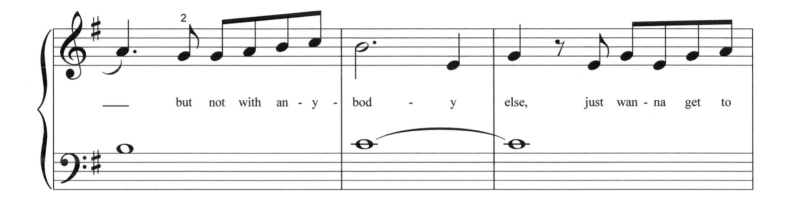

_____ but not with an - y - bod - y else, just wan - na get to

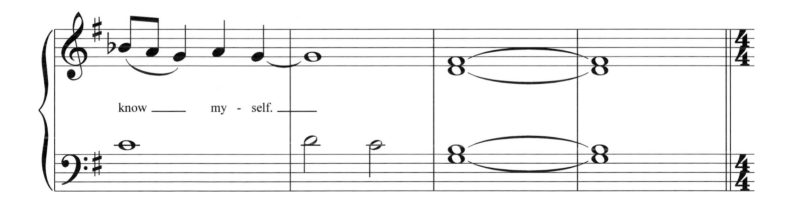

know _____ my - self. _____

Moderate Pop groove

I know, sup - pos - ed - ly, I'm lone - ly now, _____ know I'm sup-posed to be un-

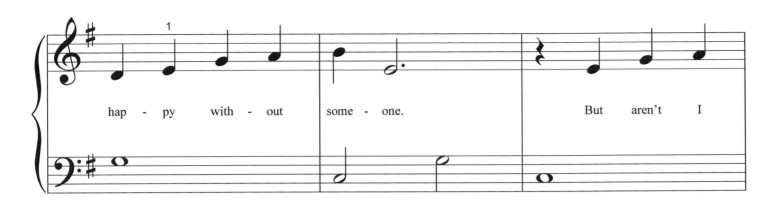

hap - py with - out some - one. But aren't I

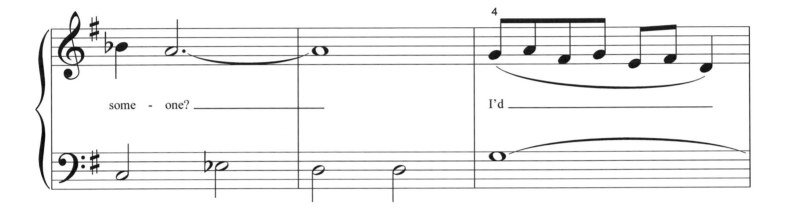

some - one? _____ I'd _____

(I'd) _____ like _____ to be your

an - swer. _____ 'Cause you're so hand - some. _____ But

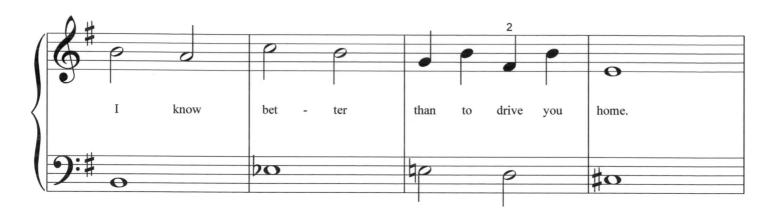

I know bet - ter than to drive you home.

'Cause you'd in - vite me in and I'd be

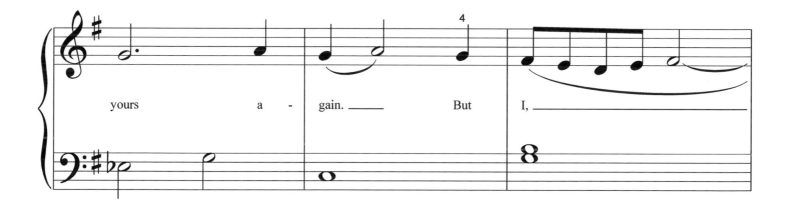

yours a - gain. _____ But I, _____

_____ I'm in love _____ with my

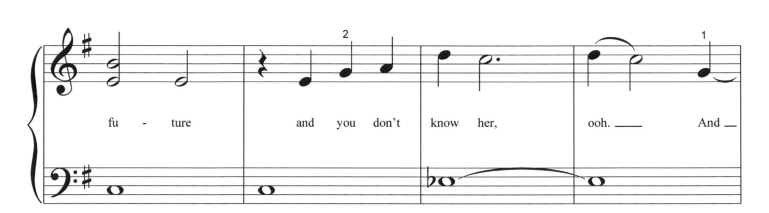

fu - ture   and you don't   know her,   ooh. ____   And __

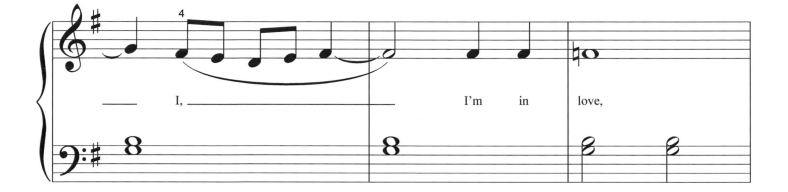

____ I, _____   I'm in love,

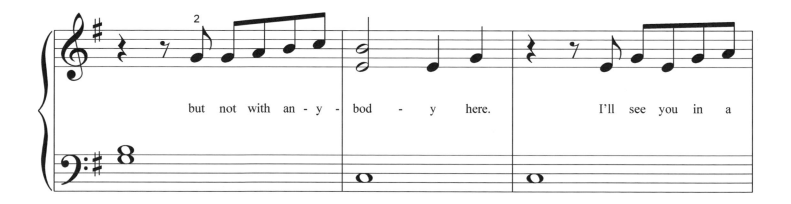

but not with an - y - bod - y here.   I'll see you in a

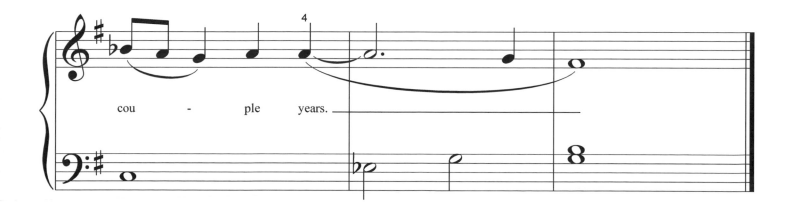

cou - ple years. _____

NO TIME TO DIE

from NO TIME TO DIE

Words and Music by BILLIE EILISH O'CONNELL
and FINNEAS O'CONNELL

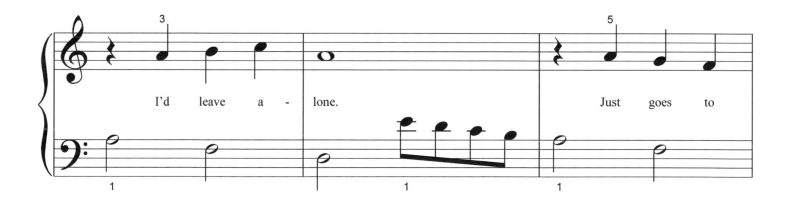

We were a pair, _____ but I saw you

there, too much to bear. _____ You were my

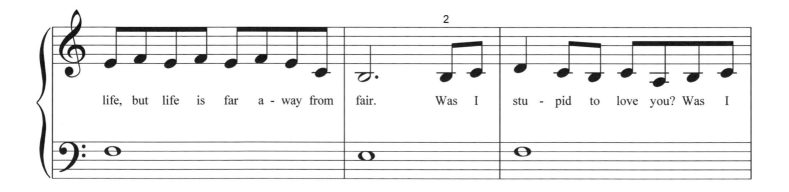

life, but life is far a-way from fair. Was I stu - pid to love you? Was I

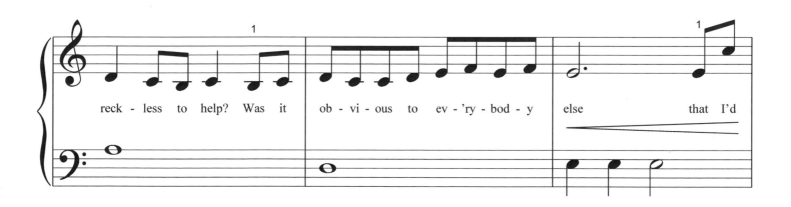

reck - less to help? Was it ob - vi - ous to ev - 'ry - bod - y else that I'd

fall - en for a lie? _____ You were nev - er on my
mf

side. _____ Fool me once, fool me twice. Are you death or par - a - dise? Now you'll

To Coda

nev - er see me cry. There's _ just no time to die.

I let it

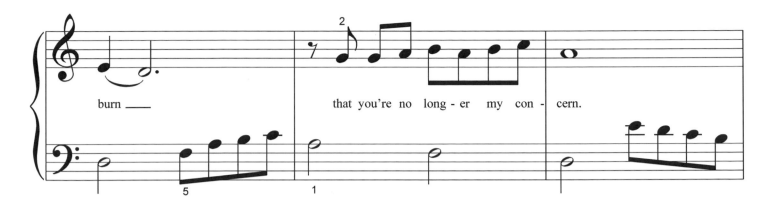

burn _____ that you're no long - er my con - cern.

Fac - es from my past re - turn, _____ an - oth - er les - son yet to

learn, that I'd

CODA

No time to

die. _____ Mm. _____ There's just no time to die.

THEREFORE I AM

Words and Music by BILLIE EILISH O'CONNELL
and FINNEAS O'CONNELL

Moderate groove

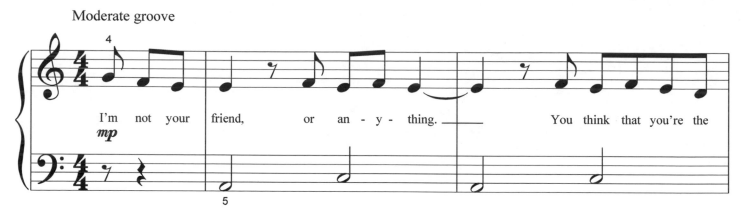

mouth.　　We are not the same, with or with - out.　　　　　　Don't

talk　'bout me like　how you might know how I　feel.　Top of the world,　but your world is - n't

real.　　　　Your world's an i - deal.　　　So,　go have

fun.　　I real - ly could - n't care less, and you can　give 'em my best, but just know, I'm not your

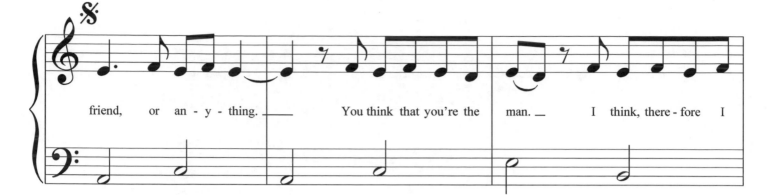

friend, or an-y-thing. ___ You think that you're the man. ___ I think, there-fore I

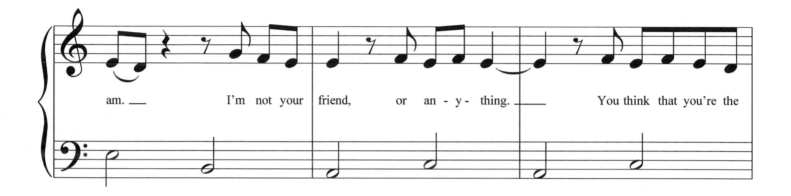

am. ___ I'm not your friend, or an-y-thing. ___ You think that you're the

To Coda

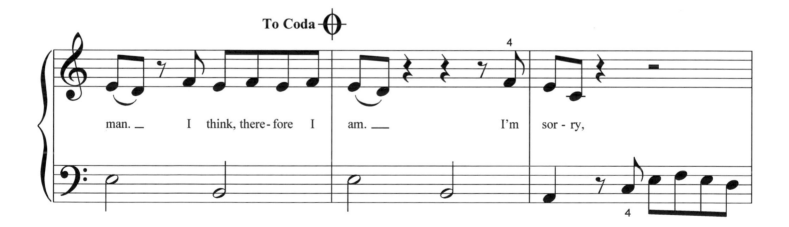

man. ___ I think, there-fore I am. ___ I'm sor-ry,

I don't think I caught your name. I'm

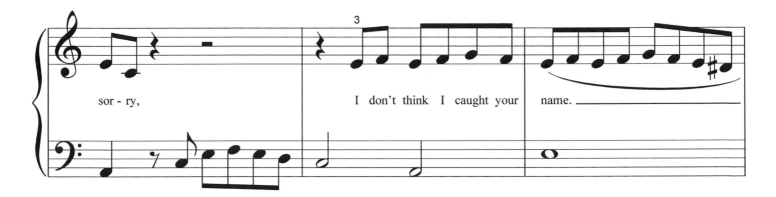

sor - ry,   I don't think I caught your   name. _____

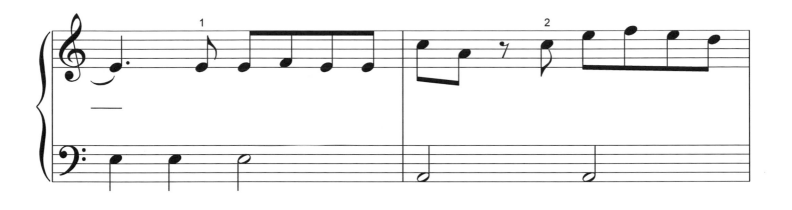

D.S. al Coda

CODA

I'm not your

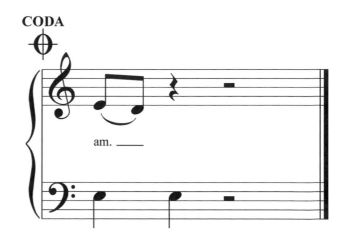

am. _____

WHEN THE PARTY'S OVER

Words and Music by
FINNEAS O'CONNELL

Gently, with motion

Don't   you   know   I'm   no   good   for   you? _____
Don't   you   know   too   much   al -   read - y? _____

I've learned to lose you,
I'll on - ly hurt you

can't af - ford to.
if you let me.

Tore my shirt to stop you bleed - ing.
Call me friend, but keep me clos - er.

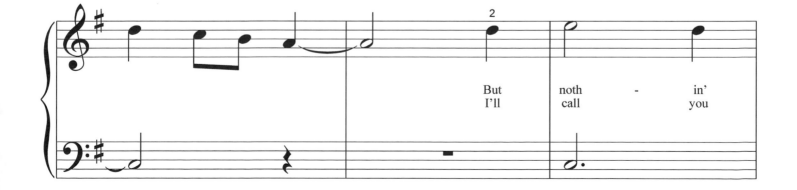

But noth - in'
I'll call you

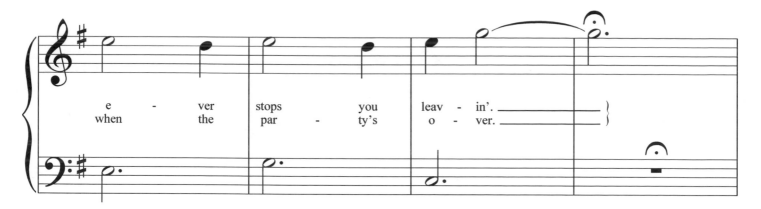

e - ver stops you leav - in'. ____
when the par - ty's o - ver. ____

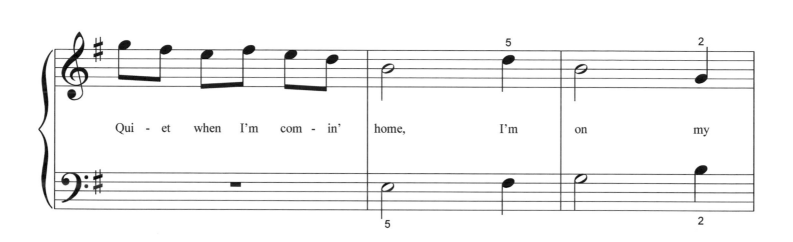

Qui - et when I'm com - in' home, I'm on my

own. I could lie, say I

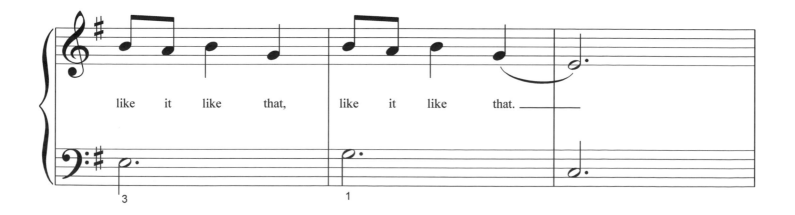

like it like that, like it like that. ____

I could lie, say I like it like that,

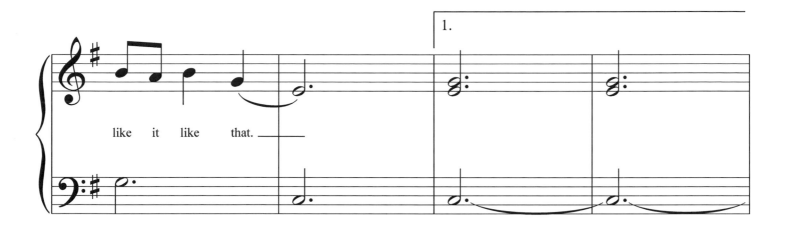

1.

like it like that.

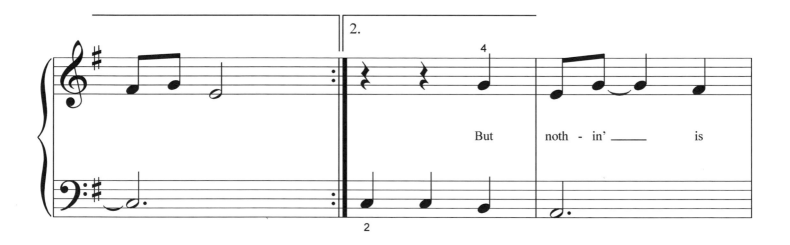

2.

But noth - in' _____ is

bet - ter _____ some - times. _____ Once we've both

said our good - byes, _____

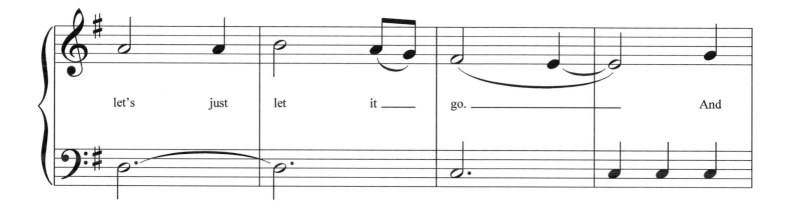

let's just let it _____ go. _____ And

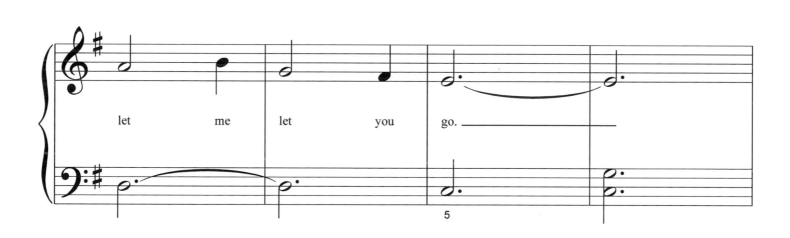

let me let you go. _____

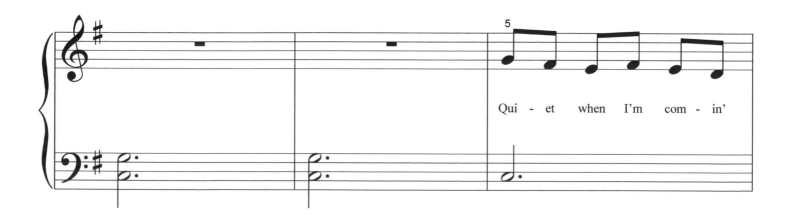

Qui - et when I'm com - in'

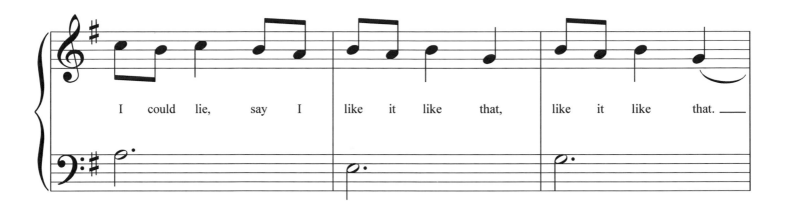

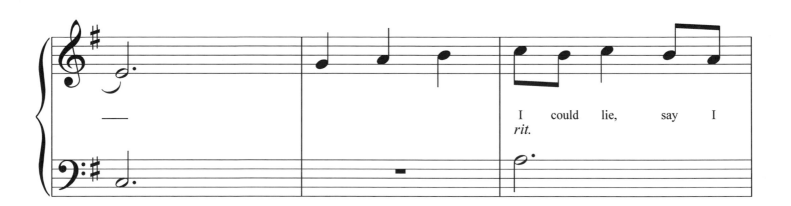

YOU SHOULD SEE ME IN A CROWN

Words and Music by BILLIE EILISH O'CONNELL
and FINNEAS O'CONNELL

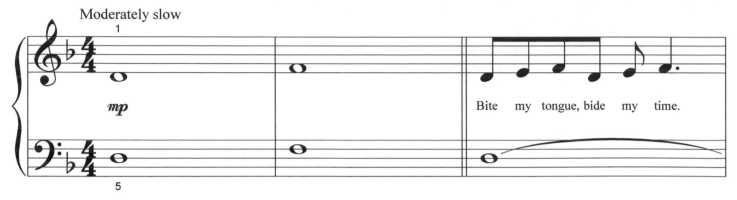

Bite my tongue, bide my time.

Wear-ing a warn-ing sign. Wait 'til the world is mine.

Vi-sions I van-dal-ize, cold in my king-dom size, fell for these o-cean eyes.

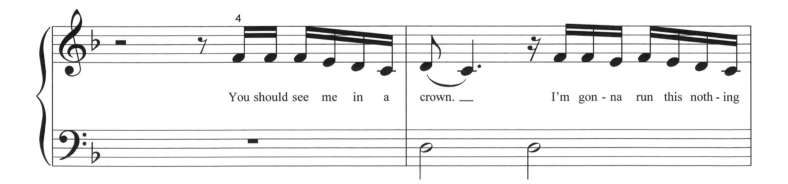

You should see me in a crown. I'm gon-na run this noth-ing

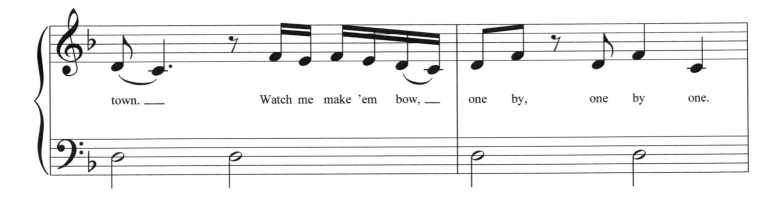

town. _____ Watch me make 'em bow, ___ one by, one by one.

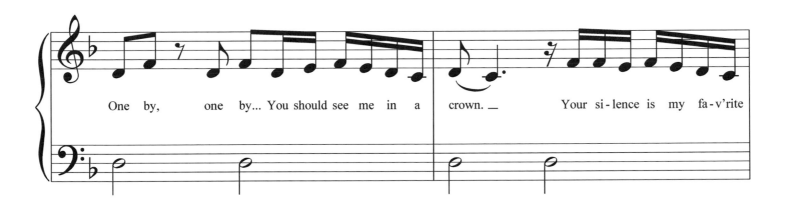

One by, one by... You should see me in a crown. ___ Your si - lence is my fa - v'rite

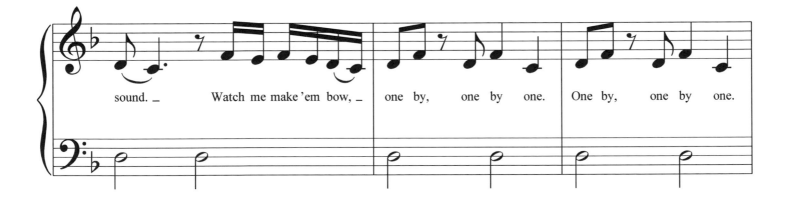

sound. _ Watch me make 'em bow, _ one by, one by one. One by, one by one.

Count my cards, watch them fall. Blood on a mar - ble wall. I like the way they all _____

46

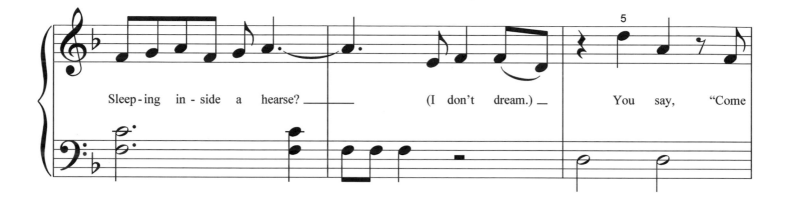

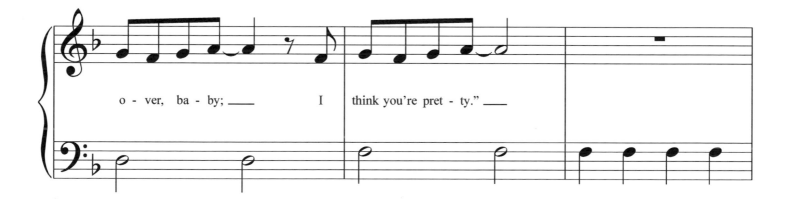

you should see me in a crown. _ I'm gon - na run this noth-ing

town. _ Watch me make 'em bow, _ one by, one by one.

One by, one by... You should see me in a crown. _ Your si - lence is my fa-v'rite

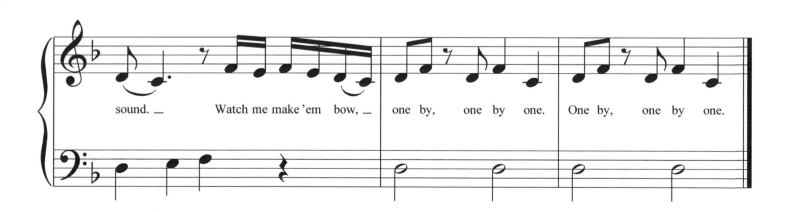

sound. _ Watch me make 'em bow, _ one by, one by one. One by, one by one.